We Can Eat the

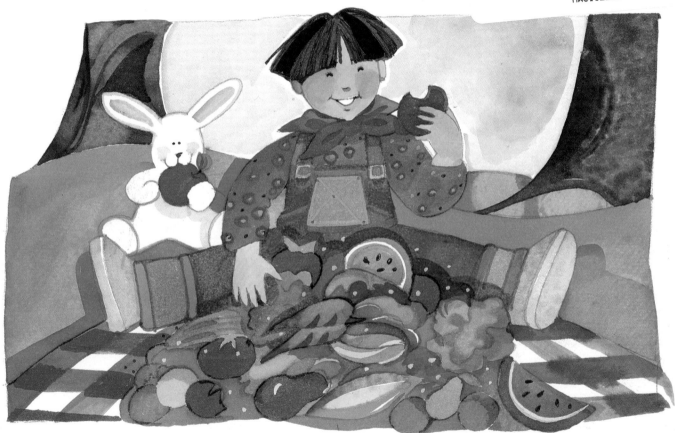

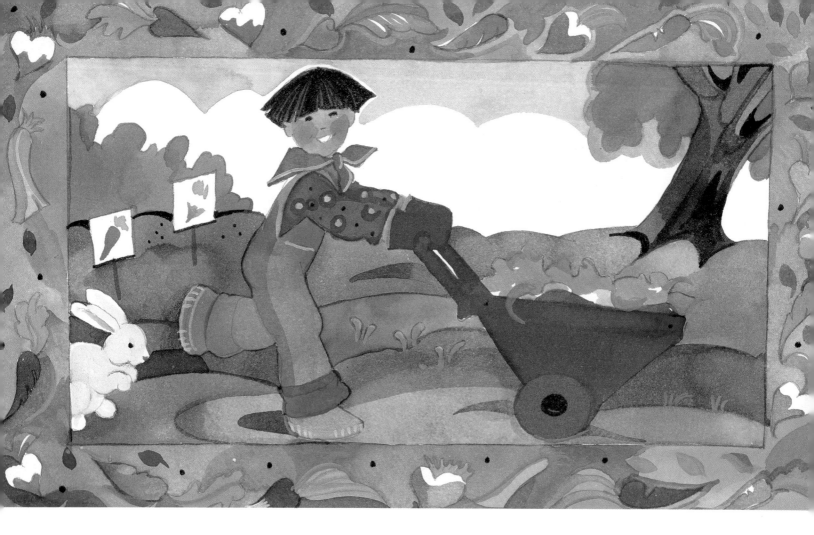

2   **We can eat the roots.**

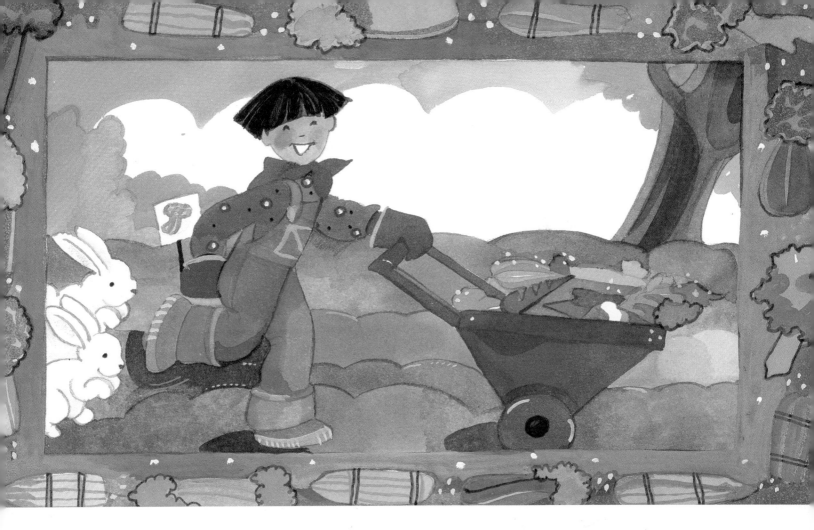

We can eat the stems.

3

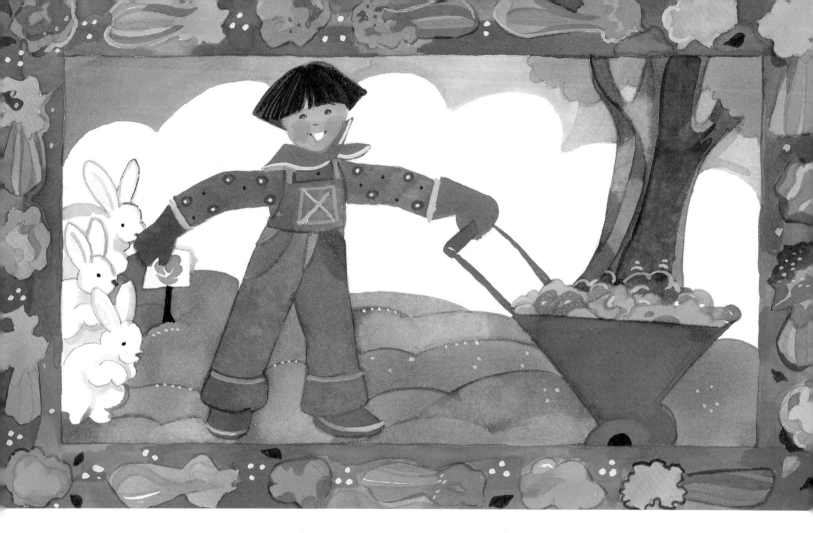

4 We can eat the leaves.

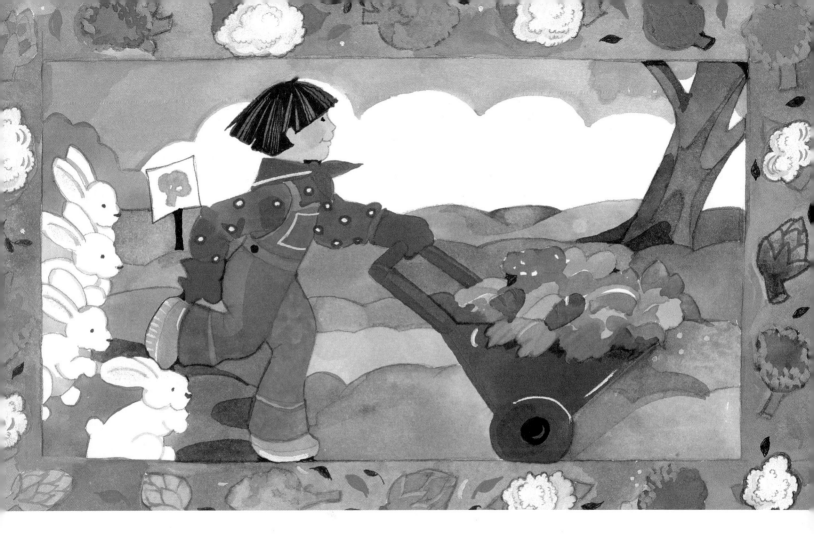

We can eat the flowers.

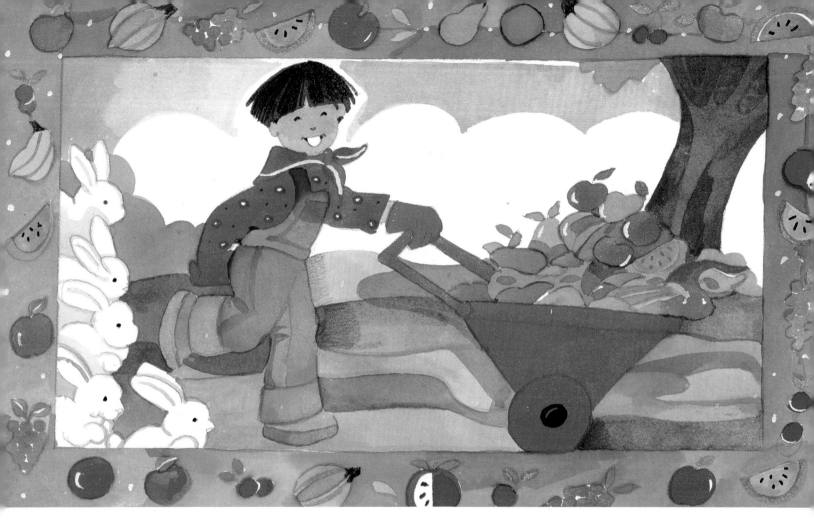

We can eat the fruit.

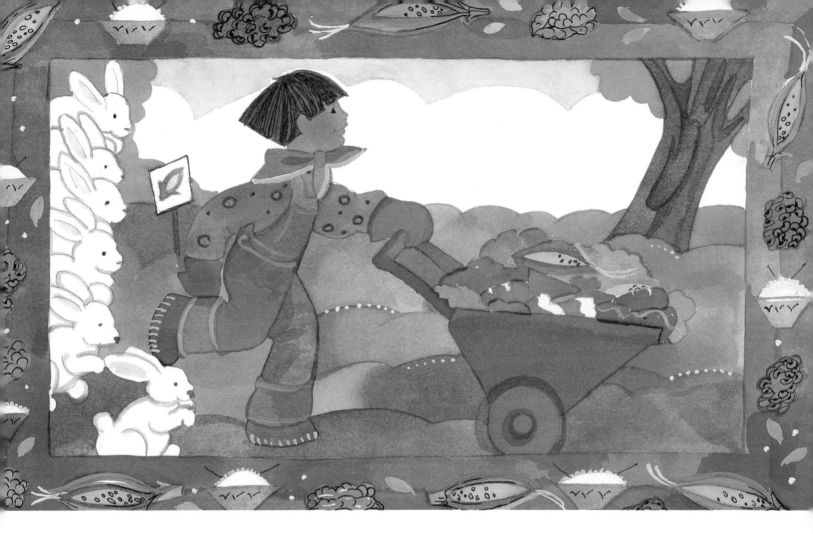

We can eat the seeds.

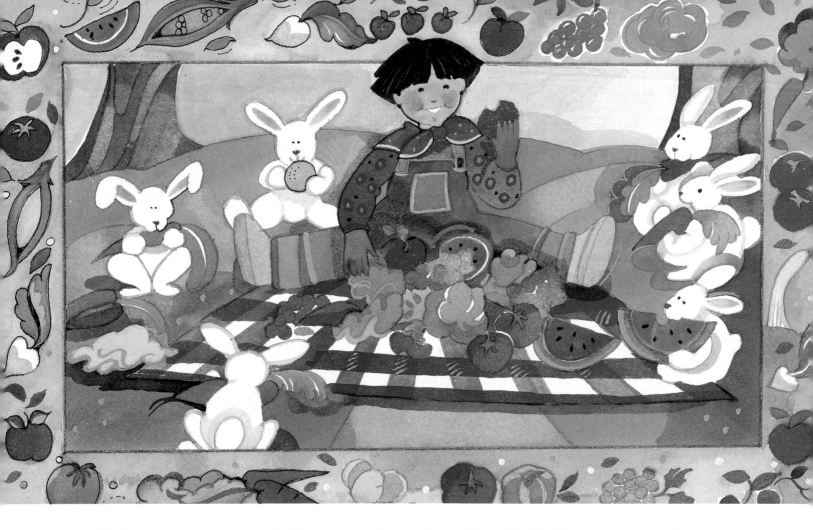

We can eat the plants. Rabbits can too!